To: Deborah —
I'm sure you've seen many of the antics in this book!
With lots of love,
Grandsam — aka — Marilyn Machog-Smith

Dec. 25/04

JACK RUSSELL TERRIERS
AND THEIR FRIENDS

JACK RUSSELL TERRIERS
AND THEIR FRIENDS

Delightful Photographs

by Marilyn Mackay-Smith

The Lyons Press
Guilford, Connecticut
An imprint of The Globe Pequot Press

To my three children: Denya, Leslie Dee, and Caroline
Without whom I probably would not have owned
Jack Russell Terriers, or bred them, or produced these photos.
This book is a reflection of their joy and love of horses,
Jack Russell Terriers, and their companions.

The Lyons Press is an imprint of The Globe Pequot Press.

The following provided photographs for the book:
Marilyn Webster, page 33
Nancy Westaway, page 69

10 9 8 7 6 5 4 3 2 1
ISBN 1-59228-434-5
Printed in China
Design by LeAnna Weller Smith

Library of Congress Cataloging-in-Publication Data is available on file.

JACK RUSSELL TERRIERS
AND THEIR FRIENDS

INTRODUCTION

I can't remember when I didn't own a camera. Someone gave me a box camera—known as a Brownie—for my sixth birthday, and I still have pictures I took with it as living proof of what was to become a lifelong hobby. Or should I say an addiction? My father was a terrific photographer and I adored him, so maybe he is partly to blame.

When selling horses became my chief source of income (I needed to put my three daughters through school), I found that the pictures I took of the horses standing and jumping were a great sales tool. I didn't have a fancy camera, but the pictures were okay. I even had good results with the cheapest Polaroid on the market. But all that was to change. It happened after I married Alex Mackay-Smith, editor of *The Chronicle of the Horse,* in 1965. At that time there were few sport-horse photographers. Soon after we were married, we traveled to England to see the U.S. Equestrian Team train for the Olympics. Alex knew that it was going to be almost impossible to get good pictures for *The Chronicle,* and this worried him.

It was then that he made a decision that would have a big impact on my life. He said, "If you can take the photos you do with that cheap Polaroid, think what you could do with a good camera." Having said that, he bought me a beautiful Nikon with two lenses. I was floored! I hadn't a clue about what to do with this fancy thing. But it started me on my "career" as a photographer, and with kind and generous help from my fellow sport photographers, who never failed to answer my questions or give me "tips," I gradually improved. I took the name "Gamecock" as my *nom de photo* after my favorite horse at the time, which seemed appropriate. It wasn't until the 1972 Munich Olympics that I started printing my own pictures. That came about thanks to Ivan Bezugloff, editor of *Dressage Magazine.* He told Alex that it was ridiculous that I didn't do my own printing and, bless him, he took it upon himself to teach me. Those who know Ivan know that when Ivan speaks, you listen, and I listened and learned and loved it. I printed all my own black and whites from then on, and it wasn't too much longer before I learned how to develop my own film.

All this led to *The Gamecock Calendar of Horses,* which I produced and sold for eighteen years. For every week of the year the calendar featured a picture of a horse along with an extended descriptive or humorous caption. This in turn led to the *Jack Russell Calendar,* which I produced for ten years. When the market became flooded with calendars, I gave them up, but I continue to be a shutterbug and always have a loaded camera near me.

My love for Jack Russell Terriers and subsequent photographing of them started with a little, nondescript rat terrier named Maxted. My daughter Caroline had met his mother, who was owned by the people whose horses she was looking after at a training session, in the summer of 1964. Caroline was ten years old, and like only a ten-year-old can, she fell in love with her. As a result we impulsively promised to get Caroline a puppy when the little dog had her next litter. Believe me, it *was* an impulse; why in the world did we need another dog? We already had a Foxhound, a Russian Wolfhound, and a German Shepherd.

A few months later, when the call came that there was a male puppy with Caroline's name on him, we were stuck. On a cold wintry morning, we took off for Unionville, Pennsylvania, and took possession of the cutest brown and white fuzz ball you ever saw. We were hooked, and whatever he was, he was special. He was intelligent, funny, and, although built incorrectly according to any terrier standard, full of personality, a great hunter (rats ceased to be a stable nuisance), never a problem despite his utter fearlessness, and best of all, Caroline's constant companion.

Sadly, he met his end protecting another dog—his lady love—from a pack of male suitors at an adjacent farm. It couldn't have come at a worse time. Caroline was very ill with both mononucleosis and a serious kidney infection. We felt that her recovery would be slowed down by this tragedy, so we made a life-changing decision. In England the previous summer, we had visited the Duke of Beaufort's hunt kennels. The kennel huntsman, Bert Pateman, took us to see his terriers, and we were really impressed with them. We phoned him, and he said he had a very good female (we wanted a male) that we *had* to have.

A friend in England agreed to take her to London Airport. One morning soon after, we received a partial telegram that said simply, "Terrier sent to Dulles [airport] today"—no flight number, no time, and no airline. We made many calls to find out which planes were due from London, England, that day. We didn't even know from which airport he had been sent. Finally, we were told that one flight did have animals on board, but the airline had no idea what kind.

Off we went. Caroline so excited she could hardly breathe. When we got to the cargo area, we still didn't know whether our terrier was on board because the cargo that arrived was literally a busload of monkeys. But wait! What was in that kennel? Sure enough, there was our white terrier, completely unimpressed by the chattering monkeys, airport noises, car smells, and the like. However, she was not the cute little puppy we expected. She was white, fully grown, and perfectly made—in short, beautiful. It took fewer than five minutes for Caroline to get over her "but it's not a puppy" disappointment, and she and the dog bonded quickly. Tempest, as Caroline named her, soon became her special friend and companion. Tempest died quietly in her sleep at fourteen years of age, leaving us as she had lived—a perfect lady.

When my daughter Denya graduated from high school in 1967, all she asked for was a Jack Russell Terrier puppy! It just so happened that a classmate of hers had a litter of newborn pups, so we capitulated and agreed she could have one. A few days later she arrived holding in one hand something that looked like a stuffed toy plucked out of F.A.O. Schwarz's window. She named him Slurpy, after the drink. No, he wasn't a show dog, but he had a lot to offer. He put great heads on my terriers, still prevalent in my breeding today, and gave them marvelous dispositions. He was intelligent, savvy, and a superb hunter. So with no initial plans to breed any dogs, we eventually became breeders of Jack Russell Terriers. Our little kennel of two was soon to be enlarged by one, when my middle daughter Leslie was given a beautiful bitch from our first litter. We were in business, like it or not!

There is no question that the Jack Russell Terrier is the dog of the decade. He has appeared in such movies as "The Mask" and "My Dog Skip." You can be sure that if you watch television for a whole evening, you're bound to see one in a commercial, not to mention on shows such as *Frasier* and *Wishbone*. The problem is that the dog you see in the movies and on television does not show the essence of the true Jack Russell Terrier.

What then *is* the true Jack Russell Terrier? He is a law unto himself. He's intelligent, happy, eager to please, and loving. He is an outdoors dog that has more energy than the Energizer Bunny. A terrific and obsessed small-game hunter, he will give up any rules he has been taught to follow this instinct. After hunting comes a love of exercise, but be aware that he is not a backyard dog. How many times do I hear, "I have a big fenced-in yard to play in"? But that's not good enough. A Jack Russell Terrier wants to *run*. If he has plenty of opportunities to hunt and to run, and if he possesses a basically good temperament, he will be the perfect house dog.

With regard to temperament, so much depends on breeding. Due to all the publicity, Jack Russell Terriers are being indiscriminately bred, and there are a lot of hyper, scrappy, yappy, cat-killing terriers available. However, if you deal with a recognized breeder, after checking with people who have bought dogs from that breeder, you are on your way to finding a wonderful friend and companion.

The Jack Russell Terrier is quick to learn and does not need a heavy hand. Take him walking, running, camping, riding, canoeing, and swimming, or on short or long car rides. Whatever you do, he will want to join in. But beware, you will find this little guy is as loving as a teddy bear with a heart as big as a lion. He will worm his way into your whole being, and you will find that you can't imagine life without him. There is no other dog, big or small, that is his equal.

I am a breeder, and as I write I have no idea how many Jack Russell Terriers I have contributed to the world, but it has to be close to a thousand. Nor do I have any idea how many photos I have taken of them. They have been recorded at play and at work; with horses, goats, sheep, and snakes (not a good idea); and while rough-housing, digging for shellfish, racing, swimming, canoeing, asleep with babies, and posing for Christmas cards.

They have never failed to join in the fun during the Christmas card sessions, acting their parts with poise and wagging their tails. We have pictures of them sitting at a table writing to Santa Claus, riding in a cart drawn by a Bouvier de Flandres, going gift shopping, eating Christmas dinner (a biscuit on each plate, which they didn't touch until we gave permission), singing carols around a piano, waiting for Santa to come down the chimney, and lying in bed sound asleep with empty stockings hanging above them.

My serious equestrian photography and my love for these terriers were a happy combination for my camera, and the reason why I never lost the impulse to take more and more Jack Russell Terrier photos. I hope you will enjoy the result of this compulsion as much as I have.

Marilyn Mackay-Smith
December 2003

Terriers are quite convinced that all
terriers are not only beautiful but are the most
expert of all, because they know that to get the best
out of Man they must not only be kind but also be
firm, and therefore handle the Man with a very
firm paw indeed—the little steel paw in the
little velvet glove—and sometimes with the help
of the little steel teeth as well.

—John Tickner

What dogs? These
are my children,
little people with fur
who make my heart
open a little wider.

—Oprah Winfrey

Every dog has his day.

—Miguel de Cervantes

It's funny how dogs and cats know

the inside of folks better than other folks do, isn't it?

—Eleanor H. Porter

You think dogs will not be in heaven?

I tell you, they will be there long before any of us.

—Robert Louis Stevenson

Dogs are not our whole lives,

but they make our lives whole.

—Roger Caras

Old age means realizing you will

never own all the dogs you wanted to.

—Joe Gores

A dog is one of
the remaining
reasons why some
people can be
persuaded to go
for a walk.

—O. A. Battista

I think we are drawn to dogs because
they are the uninhibited creatures we might be
if we weren't certain we knew better.

—George Bird Evans

Our dogs, like our shoes, are comfortable.
They might be a little bit out of shape and a little worn
around the edges, but they fit well.

—Bonnie Wilcox

Then drink puppy drink,

And let every puppy drink

That is old enough to lap and to swallow;

For he'll grow into a hound,

So we'll pass the bottle 'round,

And merrily we'll whoop and we'll hollow.

—"Drink Puppy Drink"

There is no secret so
close as that between a
rider and his horse.

—Robert Smith Surtees

Nature teaches beasts to know their friends.

—William Shakespeare

What counts is not necessarily the size of the dog in the fight—it's the size of the fight in the dog.

—Dwight D. Eisenhower

Scratch a dog and you'll find a permanent job.

—Franklin P. Jones

Happiness is a warm puppy.

—Charles Schultz

Whoever said you can't buy happiness

forgot little puppies.

—Gene Hill

I think dogs are
the most amazing
creatures; they give
unconditional love. For
me, they are the role
model for being alive.

—Gilda Radner

No man can be condemned for owning a dog.

As long as he has a dog, he has a friend;

and the poorer he gets, the better friend he has.

—Will Rogers

The dog has seldom been successful in
pulling man up to its level of sagacity, but man
has frequently dragged a dog down to his.

—James Thurber

It is fatal to let any dog

know that he is funny,

for he immediately loses

his head and starts

hamming it up.

—P. G. Wodehouse

Every dog is a lion at home.

—H. G. Bohn

A door is what a dog is perpetually on the wrong side of.

—Ogden Nash

The dog has an enviable mind;

it remembers the nice things in life and

quickly blots out the nasty.

—Barbara Woodhouse

An animal's eyes have the power to speak a great language.

—Martin Buber

Outside of a dog, a book is a man's best friend.

And inside of a dog, it's too dark to read.

—Groucho Marx

If you want a friend in Washington, get a dog.

—Harry Truman

Fox terriers are born with about
four times as much original sin in them
as other dogs are, and it will take years
and years of patient effort on the part of
us Christians to bring about any appreciable
reformation in the rowdiness
of the fox-terrier nature.

—Jerome K. Jerome

The fidelity of a dog is a precious gift
demanding no less binding moral responsibilities
than the friendship of a human being.

—Konrad Lorenz

A dog is just a
kid with fur.

—Anonymous

The average dog is a nicer person than the average person.

—Andy Rooney

To his dog, every man is Napoleon;
hence the constant popularity of dogs.

—Aldous Huxley

Outspeak the Squire:

"Give room I pray,

And hie the terriers in;

The warriors of the fight are they,

And every fight they win."

—Ring Ouzel

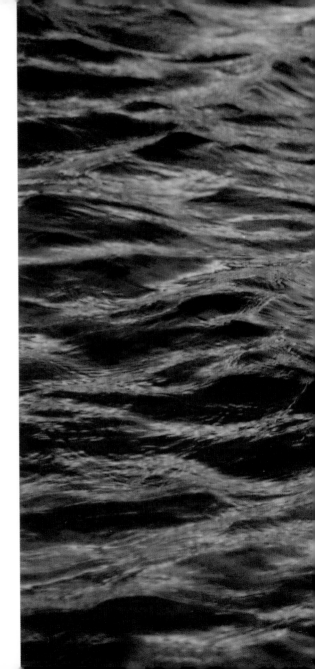

A dog in a kennel
barks at his fleas;
a dog hunting does
not notice them.

—Chinese proverb

The trouble with a cuddly pup

Is eventually he's a dog grown up.

—Marilyn Mackay-Smith (with apologies to Ogden Nash)

Most terriers are independent,

tough dogs with a predisposition to bark when excited

(and they get excited very easily).

—Stanley Coren

The dog was created specially for children.

He is the god of frolic.

—Henry Ward Beecher

Dogs display reluctance and wrath

If you try to give them a bath.

They bury bones in hideaways

And half the time they trot sideaways.

—Ogden Nash

A dog is the only thing on this earth that
loves you more than he loves himself.

—Josh Billings

Puppies are nature's remedy for feeling unloved . . .

plus numerous other ailments of life.

—Richard Allan Palm

True happiness consists not in the multitude
of friends, but in their worth and choice.

—Samuel Johnson

There is no faith which has never yet been broken,

except that of a truly faithful dog.

—Konrad Lorenz

My little dog—

a heartbeat at my feet.

—Edith Wharton

The greatest pleasure of a dog is that you may
make a fool of yourself with him, and not only will he not
scold you, but he will make a fool of himself too.

—Samuel Butler

One dog barks at something—the rest bark at him.

—Chinese proverb

If having a soul means being able to feel
love and loyalty and gratitude, then animals
are better off than a lot of humans.

—James Herriot

One of the most
popular is undoubtedly
the fox terrier. This is
assuredly the doggiest
dog we possess, the
most aggressive,
born to trouble as the
sparks fly upward.

—W. H. Hudson

Dogs lead a nice life.

You never see a dog with a wristwatch.

—George Carlin

The reason a dog has so many friends is that
he wags his tail instead of his tongue.

—Anonymous

Dogs wait for us faithfully.

—Marcus Tullius Cicero